THE KESTREL IN THE CRANE

Acknowledgements

Thanks to Newcastle Chronicle and Journal for their kind permission to reproduce pages from The Evening Chronicle, 1953.

Illustrations and photographs ©Rod Alder unless otherwise indicated. Unless indicated that they are by James Alder, illustrations are by Rod Alder.

©Rod Alder, 2014
Published by
City of Newcastle upon Tyne
Newcastle Libraries
Tyne Bridge Publishing, 2014
www.tynebridgpublishing.co.uk
www.newcastle.gov.uk/libraries

ISBN 978-185795-220-9

In 1965 James Alder designed this kestrel logo for the RSPB Young Ornithologists' Club. It was adapted to become their badge.

Printed by Statex Colourprint, Newcastle upon Tyne

THE KESTREL IN THE CRANE

Rod Alder

based on an original story by James Alder

Tyne Bridge Publishing

EVENING CHRONICLE, Friday, June 5, 1953

Ma Kestrel finds a shipyard home

She kicked out the rooks from a wire nest

By JAMES ALDER, the noted "Evening Chronicle" Naturalist.

AS our towns and industrial centres spread into the surrounding countryside many creatures of the wild are having to relinquish their traditional homes.

Fields, woods, hedges and marshes are engulfed by brick and cement. Even cliffs and gullies, once inaccessible because of their distance from towns, are not safe places for wild life, for cheap transport and the popularity of rock climbing have made many of these spots too unhealthy for some of the more timid creatures.

But nature is not to be beaten and observers note that the birds and beasts are rehabilitating themselves. Kittiwake gulls, which are sea cliff dwellers, have nested on the ledges of warehouses by the river. The rare black redstart has nested in the ruins of bombed houses in London. Hares find that airfields are safe abodes and they treat the comings and goings of aircraft quite nonchalantly.

Much of my time this season has been spent in searching for the nest of the kestrel, that lovely little hawk which is commonly seen hovering over the fields and hedges as it searches for mice. I failed to find one until a bird-watching friend who is employed in a famous shipyard told me that a pair were nesting in a tower crane in his yard.

First I had to get permission to investigate this report and to my surprise and delight I was given every assistance. I had hardly hoped that the builders of great ships would bother about a bird's nest, but the results speak for themselves.

The nest was situated on a girder under the machine room on the swinging boom of the crane, with a sheer drop of approximately 140 feet to the ground. Originally this nest had been built by a pair of rooks, and indeed the rooks had laid their complement of eggs when the kestrels, after a tussle, took over. When I first saw it, the nest contained six red-brown kestrel eggs and one green, speckled rook's. I had hoped to photograph this unusual sight, but when I returned with my camera the hen kestrel had destroyed the last rook's egg.

The rooks, it seems, having decided to nest in a shipyard had made up their minds to compete with the human builders for engineering honours. They built their nest almost entirely of wire. Yes, they made it of pieces of cable, packing case wire, and welding wires, binding some of their ends so securely round the girders that nothing short of an earthquake will shift it. See how adaptable nature is!

But back to the kestrels. The hen kestrel was sitting her eggs fairly tightly and it was possible to walk along the catwalk to within eight feet of her before she left her nest, when she would fly around the crane and swoop at me to scare me away.

She took to my "hide" quickly and at the click of my camera shutter meant nothing to her. She was too used to the clang and clamour of the yard to bother with a triviality. Normally when I am bird-watching I am more used to the signing of the wind through heather and the plaintive cries of moorland birds, and I found the grinding crash of the huge gears in the machine room behind me almost unbearable; but the kestrel brooded her eggs unconcernedly.

The great crane lifted tons of prefabricated sections, swung slowly and dropped them into position. The great hulk of ship below acquired a set of ribs and a prow. But the kestrel thought nothing of these marvels. She had eggs to hatch.

I hope to show you in two or three weeks' time the result of her patience—and mind. I hope also to show you then, the kestrel, mouse catcher! But, "The best laid plans of mice and men . . . . ."

Here the hen kestrel has just returned to the nest and is about to settle on her six eggs. Close examination of the photograph will show that the nest is made almost entirely of wire.

140 feet above ground is my canvas hide shown as a small white square against the dark machine room on the end of the boom. The nest is eight feet away from the hide, on a girder opposite the hide.

Reproduced from The Evening Chronicle, 5 June, 1953.

1

There where the rusty iron lies,
The rooks are cawing all the day.
Perhaps no man until he dies,
Will understand them, what they say.

Rooks, Charles Hamilton Sorley

The rook strutted to the end of the girder that projected from the corner of the great workshop and surveyed the scene below with a beady eye. A light breeze ruffled the baggy plumage about his thighs, feathers glistening in the pale March sunlight. Bowing low, he spread his rounded tail, uttering a raucous caw that resounded and echoed round the corrugated roof of the building.

This was a far cry from where he had been born, in a large rookery in the tall elms over a grey church in Ovingham where his call would have caused a great stirring in the tree tops. That was four springs ago. Here in the shipyard, the noise was

deafening with the
sound of pneumatic
riveters and the little
engines shunting their
trucks, interspersed
with the crashing of
metal plates and the
hissing of electric
welders, showering
bright, crackling sparks
from their fiery tongues.

But the rook felt quite at home here; the clamour meant no
more to him than it did to the craftsmen below, protected by
their goggles from the intense glare of their torches, skilfully
drawing lines of molten metal down the butt-joint of two steel
plates high on the ship's hull. This was the object of the rook's
excitement. Quickly, the welding rod in the man's left hand
burned down to a stub, dropping to the ground some thirty
feet below.

The moment for which the rook had waited arrived. He
hurled himself into the air and with wing tips spread like
fingers he wheeled to the ground and landed with a triple
bounce. Waddling over to the fallen rod he stabbed out with
his rapier bill to nip up the shiny metal then quickly rose on
strongly beating wings. Up he flew on the strong updraught
between the two steel walls into the girder of crane No. 8.

A hundred and forty feet above the ground he was
raucously greeted by his mate as his claws rattled on an L-
sectioned girder on the great jib. Four bounding hops from
crossbeam to crossbeam carried him to the end of the jib
where he stood on her nest below the engine house. And what

a nest – not since the swallows had deserted the cliffs to nest under eaves had such a sensation in nests been created. It was made entirely of wire. Packing case wires with twisted ends; flat wire strips that had bound heavy screw boxes; pieces of cable and welding rods of all lengths; some new and shining like silver, all securely inter-twined and bound about the girder so that nothing short of an earthquake would shift it.

The rooks exchanged bows, fanned tails, and he offered the female the stubby rod which she accepted and tucked among the twisted mass. He offered her make-believe food which she pretended to accept, then, with a throaty cry, she hurled herself off into a magnificent glide over the Tyne, followed a second later by her mate.

Together, they swung down river then back to the north bank where they had spotted a squabble at the end of the yard. Here a battle royal was in progress around a giant crane, a monster that could lift a whole ship's prow at one go. Five shapes, three black like themselves and two pinky-brown ones – the kestrels.

At the end of the yard, two pairs of rooks nested on the

giant. Both had wire nests, for trees do not grow in shipyards and wire was just as good, if not better, than sticks and twigs.

Gleefully, the two rooks hurled themselves into the melée, knocking the male kestrel off balance into the forest of girders. The female kestrel had gained four hundred feet in height from the impetus of a mighty swoop, dropping on one wing and peeling off slowly into a breathtaking dive. The slipstream from her swoop buffeted all five rooks as she shot among them at seventy miles an hour, scattering the ragged, cawing mob, but only for a moment, for they returned noisily into the fray with true communal spirit.

From below, the ship workers looked up from their dinner-time domino game in amazement as the two species made fullest use of the treacherous air currents above the giant.

The battle swirled on but not an injury was sustained. Then as suddenly as it had begun, the kestrels broke off the fight. A half hearted chase by the rooks did not last long and over the south bank one of the rooks got her eye on a bunch of straw sticking out of a packing case. The last touch of luxury for the nest.

She and her mate dropped down onto a wooden fence, one keeping lookout while the other stole the straw and then together they flew back across the moored tugs and tankers to the far bank.

2

… the mastery of the thing!
The Windhover, Gerard Manley Hopkins

Down-river, at three hundred feet, the kestrel pair winnowed above grimy fields where unkempt cart ponies grazed down to the water's edge. Rough grassy banks backed the riverside buildings where the kestrels found good hunting.

They circled, dropped to a hundred and twenty feet and took their seats on the light west wind. Now they showed the true mastery of flight that earned them their name, 'windhover'; facing the breeze with wings widely spread, head dropped, tail fanned and feet bunched at exactly the point of balance, they remained motionless for seconds at a time. A vagary in the wind that upset their balance needed just a quiver of the wing tips to reset the delicate poise and keep them in a position where they could survey the ground below with nature's keenest eyesight.

Movement was what they sought and when their eyes failed to detect life below they slipped sideways to cover a new strip of ground, and with the flick of a wing tip, rebalanced themselves on the wind.

Suddenly the male kestrel teetered forward and slid obliquely down, strong talons swinging below and wings and tail streaming in the slipstream. Appearing to strike the rough grass without braking was an illusion. At the last moment, he brought his wings down with a powerful stroke that broke his fall and at the same time hooded his prey to prevent its escape. The little vole made a frantic scamper for its grassy tunnel... but too late! Needle-sharp talons struck it.

Meanwhile, his mate had her eye on slightly bigger game. A half grown rat had slid below a black weedy jetty and was swimming like a small otter towards a mud bank that led to

crumbling stone stairs. Climbing out of the water, the rat paused and nosed the air with trembling whiskers, then ambled over the mud leaving dainty star-shaped prints on the surface. Half way across, where the rat reached a few slimy stones embedded in the mud, the kestrel struck. The struggle ended almost immediately. A quick end was important to the kestrel's survival.

Once he had eaten, the male rose from his high post and winnowed over the river. Far below, with his mate still feeding on the tip of the warehouse roof, he felt the urge to impress, diving like a bullet towards her. Faster and faster he travelled until it seemed certain that he would strike her. Then at the last moment his wings flicked open and his tail ruddered him, his wing tip just brushing her. Again and again he plunged until she launched herself from the roof and climbed swiftly with him.

When they were but two little crosses in the sky, they swung away from each other, each drawing half of a figure of eight, then curved gracefully and converged to the figure's centre where they closed as one. With talons clasped and wings raised in angelic fashion, they spiralled down in a crazy aerial waltz until it seemed that their madness would end in a watery grave. But, just in time they parted and winged across the swirling river to swing up to the top of the giant crane's huge arm.

In the shadow of the girders, both birds sat quietly, but very much aware of the rook squatting on her nest in the corner of the jib.

Gliding silently down the centre of the jib, weaving in and out the diagonal struts, the female kestrel landed with a click of talons on a fish plate six feet away from the rook. The placid rook flattened herself and glared at the kestrel with her beak open uttering frightened pantings.

Suddenly a ragged black bomb hurtled through the girders and sent the kestrel flying and within seconds, the sky was filled with swirling birds fighting around the giant, its great arm swinging impassively with the tanker's engine hanging from its cables.

Winded by the encounter, both kestrels flew off down river for three miles where they sat meditatively on the roof of the Venerable Bede's church.

Days passed, and the female rook had just laid her sixth egg, completing the clutch of smooth, greenish mottled eggs. Suddenly she was faced with the frightening apparition of a female kestrel on the girder beside her. Confused and frightened, the rook took flight, only to be chased by the kestrel's mate who had been watching from above the crane.

Triumphantly, the female kestrel hopped across to the vacated rook's nest and clutched its wire rim in her tense, possessive talons.

3

Build me a straight, O worthy Master!
Stanch and strong, a goodly vessel,
That shall laugh at all disaster,
And with wave and whirlwind wrestle!

The Building of the Ship, Henry Wadsworth Longfellow

It was 19th April and the kestrel had just laid her first egg, blotched with red and brown among the rook's six greenish ones. Rising from the clutch, she bowed and rocked from one leg to the other. Nudging one of rook's eggs with her hooked bill she pierced the shell and carried it to the edge of the nest where it was released, watching it curiously as it dropped away. A shout of derisive laughter was heard from the squad of men below as the egg just missed a welder, splattering on the steel deck of the skeletal ship. Eggs were laid at two day intervals, and each time a rook's egg was tipped overboard. When the third egg was laid, she settled on them to warm them through until she finally completed the clutch, a total of six.

A ship's carpenter had been observing the kestrels with interest for some time during his dinner breaks. His friend James Alder was an ornithologist and photographer, so the carpenter informed James of the goings on at crane No. 8. Much to James's amazement, after seeking permission from the shipyard owners, he was given permission to study the kestrels up in the crane.

First he needed some information about the birds and the yard and was directed, along with the carpenter, to a large man, a joiner, who knew exactly where the kestrels were located. Leading the way up the crazy vertical climb, the hefty workman just squeezed through the hatches in the crane's ascending stages until they reached the narrow catwalk of the swinging jib.

As they walked along the catwalk the kestrel flung herself off the nest and hurtled beneath the jib, then flew up and over with an angry outburst of cries.

'Fierce isn't she?' said the man.

'Did she nest here last year?' asked the photographer.

'Aye, she did that.'

'And how did she get on? Did the young fledge successfully?'

'Well, as a matter of fact,' said the man, 'aa was up here one day, and as aa watched the hen bringing little birds to feed her young'uns, why it was cruel watching her pullin' them to pieces and givin' them ti her little'uns. So aa got a lang stick, and aa swept them aall off ti the groond.'

The photographer's eyes swept slowly down from the nest to the sickening void below it, and the joiner sucked strongly at his empty pipe.

Fortunately, the photographer had been trained to fly an open topped Tiger Moth aeroplane at the local airport and was used to heights, albeit in a different situation.

The catwalk between the driver's aerial cabin and the engine house was only three feet wide with a handrail down each side, but by sitting in the doorway, James could look round the corner and see the nest only nine feet away. The next problem was how to conceal his camera whilst sitting in some comfort.

The catwalk was forty feet long and its whole length could be seen by the sitting bird. A hide to conceal himself had to be constructed, as far back as possible at first, then hopefully to be moved closer once the bird became adjusted to the strange structure. A three feet square piece of canvas was fastened to the handrail at a distance, and a bright light tin lid was placed in its centre to simulate a camera lens.

On his return the next day, the crane driver told James that the kestrel had returned almost immediately to the nest, so the hide was now moved nearer to the nest while the kestrel sulked on crane No. 10. Now it was time to try out the complete hide which was made against the engine house doorway. James hid himself inside and the crane driver went back into his control box. No sooner had his boots ceased to ring on the steel catwalk than the kestrel was back on the girder next to the nest, fixing the tiny hole through which the photographer was peering with an intent stare.

Later that day, a larger hole was cut and the lens of the plate camera pushed through and mounted on a solid box inside the hide. The camera was focused critically on a ground glass screen with the aid of a magnifying glass and then a photographic plate was slid into position.

A darker object, a silent shutter which still made an audible click, had now replaced the glassy eye of the lens and went unnoticed by the bird. With the kestrel now settled on her eggs James squeezed the pneumatic bulb that operated the shutter, hoping that she would not hear the click.

Three feet above, in the engine house, the great gears crashed deafeningly as the taut cables hummed and the crane shuddered as it lifted twenty tons of prefabricated ship and swung it with precise position under the driver's skilful guidance.

Having taken his first picture, James relaxed to study the kestrel. She was mild-eyed and fluffy-feathered. Only the fiercely hooked blue bill with its fosse or notch, and yellow cere identified her as a bird of prey for her strong yellow legs and feet with their black talons were hidden below her. Talons that had torn a thousand rats and mice now caressed six tiny packages of life in shelly prisons. She had bare yellow skin around her eyes and a suggestion of a dark moustache, a chestnut-red mantle which was strongly barred with dark brown, and a long grey-pink tail, narrowly barred down its length, with a dark sub-terminal band and creamy tip. Her soft breast was pale buff with dark shaft streaks and her chin, the feathers of which bristled forward under her beak, in a curious rounded bunch, was creamy white.

For the next hour she brooded peacefully, occasionally stirring to raise herself gently to turn the eggs. James caught a glimpse of a pink-brown black and blue tail as the male shot under the jib, and the female became alert.

From the tower crane by the river's edge came an insistent

call like a creaking gate, and she opened her beak slightly and replied with a thinner higher pitched note. The male called again and she suddenly hurled herself from the nest, half-looped under the jib's main spar and winnowed across to the tower crane where she landed on the roof of the engine house next to her mate. A mouse dangled from his beak. She stretched forward and snatched it from him, then transferred it to her own talons and began to tear.

Many days of thrilling experiences followed and photography was almost forgotten in this totally new world in the sky. There were days when James was torn between watching nature in the raw and the fascinating art of shipbuilding. On one side of the crane, an Esso tanker hull was fast approaching completion and on the other, a new keel was being laid. Nearby, he could see the *City of Durban* nearing its final stages.

He marvelled at the finger tip precision as the prefabricated parts and huge chalk-marked steel plates of the new ship were gently laid. The keel then acquired a set of ribs until it looked like the skeleton of some monstrous leviathan.

Although the crane's feet were almost at water level, its jib still reared above the Tyne's steep north banks. He could see ugly prefabricated sheds and buildings sprawling round a huge gasometer, then a sea of red brick houses, churches and chimneys stretching to the soft green of distant fields. A mile seawards, where the river elbowed out of sight to the right, there were more cranes, more huge sheds and more ships.

Some days the river flowed blue, reflecting the sky. On others, without the kindly sky above, it flowed dirty yellow, grey and muddy. From Newcastle to the coast it flowed, nothing but an open sewer, spewing its contents into the North Sea.

Only the hardiest of fish could breathe in this environment, for the oxygen generated by its sweet tributaries had long been converted into killing carbon dioxide by the decaying particles of muck that clouded it, making the river almost impossible for life. It was fit for little except to bear the beautiful ships made on its banks, certainly not the silvery salmon, which, even when

James was a boy, had been caught in large numbers. Now, fewer and fewer survived the deadly run to spawn in the gravel beds of the Tyne's headwaters. A link that had gone back to prehistoric times was now being broken.

No one was to know then that the clear, sparkling waters of the Tyne's tributaries would one day again flow uninterrupted to the North Sea. Man's attitudes would change radically for the better. The disposal of the industrial and domestic waste into the Tyne would cease and the mighty river would be re-established as a haven for wildlife, and see the return of the great salmon.

James remembered the weekly fair on the Newcastle quayside each Sunday morning, where people thronged to spend their weekend pennies. The coconut shies, darts stalls and gaudy ice cream wagons, all claiming to be triple gold medal winners; cheap lemonade and sodas sold from hand carts, the smell of hundreds of chain horses; and gullible cloth-capped men crowding round shifty individuals whose gift of the gab enabled them to squeeze every penny from their audience. The fire eaters, the sword swallowers and the escapologists, covered in sores from their repeated exertions. But best of all, the little man who climbed down the iron rungs to the lapping water, hanging there with one arm, waiting for a tired salmon to wriggle along. James remembered the approach of the policeman and the man's frantic efforts to hide the salmon down his trouser leg, and the laughter as a pool of water was formed around his feet, the policemen savouring the situation before the fish slowly slid down his leg and the tail appeared by his boot!

It was another Sunday morning that prompted these memories. The yard was quiet and his boots clattered as James climbed the one hundred and forty rungs to the nest site.

The kestrel had been sitting tight on the nest and flew off at the sight of the man, swiftly returning as he hid behind the hide. Now he sat back to enjoy the strange peace of the crane. No human voices or the rasping of machines and crashing of metals.

Suddenly, he became aware of a thin hissing sound from the nest which increased to a whistle. The sound rose, shriller and louder, and the crane began to move, shuddering and swaying in a sickening motion. The jib creaked and the whole horizon seemed to swing about it; where it once had pointed west to east, it now pointed in entirely the opposite direction!

JAMES ALDER TAKES YOU AWAY FROM THE DAY'S NEWS WITH ANOTHER LOVELY STORY

MA KESTREL REARS HER 5 BABIES

Remember the remarkable photographs taken by JAMES ALDER, our noted naturalist, showing a kestrel's nest high in the tracery of a Tyneside shipyard crane? Today James Alder describes the happy sequel — the successful rearing of a new kestrel family.

By JAMES ALDER

Now thirty days old, this young kestrel sits on the girder and seems to contemplate its own launching over the shipyard.

THE kestrel successfully hatched out five of her six eggs, and, sensibly, she allowed the sixth to lie among her powder puffs of babies for two or three days before she decided to throw it out as a 'dud.'

When they were very small, she brooded the chicks to keep them warm and displayed a tenderness towards them that would surprise people, this strong maternal instinct seems stranger still in such a creature when you know something of its life history.

Here's an extract from my notebook which recorded the minute by minute events at the nest and illustrates a 'domestic' scene.

* The cock kestrel calls from a short distance away, an insistent sound like a creaking gate. The hen, brooding her restless down-covered chicks, replies with a rather thinner, higher pitched edition of his call, and raises her head feather.

* They carry on a sort of conversation which might almost be 'I have a mouse!' 'High time too—the children are hungry!' She leaves the nest and returns in a moment with a small mouse in her beak.

* The nestlings are very excited, and she stands well back from them, clutching her prey in her strong talons, and begins to rend small pieces from it. With her head to one side she delicately offers a piece to each chick, and one by one feeds them, giving them the soft pieces only, fur and all, and eats the coarse or bony pieces herself.

* Suddenly the cock returns again, this time binding on the nest. He is a lovely little bird, much smaller than the hen as is the rule among hawks. He hands over a sparrow leg to each nestling but all refuse it. She swallows it herself, and tries again with the other leg, but again she has to eat it herself.

* One by one the nestlings drop back satisfied and close their eyes as she stands over them.

* Meanwhile the crane, still working and swinging, has turned so that the sun beats down on the nest corner. The hen tries to shelter her brood from its rays but by now her family is proving more than a wingful. She droops her wings and straddles the chicks, and as they jostle and pant for a place in the shade she gasps and pants in the heat.

Soon, however, as the nestlings grow strong and their rust and brown-barred feathers peeped through their baby down, the hen was rid of this heavy family responsibility and joined her mate in the search for food. Many a young dockyard and riverside rat and mouse ended his life in her talons —and sometimes the more innocent sparrows, too.

The once tidy wire nest became foul smelling and infested with bluebottles which the young kestrels pursued and ate with obvious enjoyment. They learned to clasp the wire strands with sharp claws as they exercised their growing wings and played a sort of game of tig along the girders, panicking wildly if they lost balance and rushing back to the security of the nest platform to recover nerve.

They preened their plumage carefully to remove the irksome down, and as if to exercise the eyes that would

one day detect the movement of a beetle from two hundred feet up, they intently watched loose feathers that idled in the air currents about the girders.

Then came a day when the parents would not return to the nest. When all they did was to call from a nearby crane. What were they saying? "Here, I have a mouse for you—if you come and get it."

I saw the first youngster launch himself into the vastness below him. He dropped and teetered on the air uncertainly, and then triumphantly his winnowing wings and frantic ruddering won him control and he was

flying to circle the crane and land on the platform to me.

My very last view of the kestrel family was a ... see it in the large photos. The second eldest—he day older than the other sitting on the apparently contemplating plunge which he must make, and the others sitting somewhat glum. He got nervous about the "solo" you know!

One of the fledglings a bad job of his first dive and landed in a pool of ... He is now in my possession looking very bedraggled. I hope that one day he will fly again.

Covered in blue-grey down, the nestlings are just a few days old. Here they are eagerly lining up before the hen as she prepares to feed them.

The first flight accomplished, this fledgling kestrel sits proudly on the handrail of the catwalk at the top of the crane.

You don't know half of it
— until you have read

CHRISTIE'S OWN STORY

by
Christie himself

NEW BOOKS

Maintenance to map reading, routes and records, interesting cycling facts and everyday problems are expertly covered in the 400 pages of "Every Cyclists' Pocket Book" by F. J. Camm (G. Newnes, 5s.).

"The Wonderful Country," an illustrated novel by Tom Lea (Heinemann, 15s.)—set in the borderlands of Mexico and Texas, tells the adventures of Martin Brady, a paid pistolero. First-class writing.

"All Very Regular," by Victor Bridges (Macdonald, 9s 6d)—an exciting story of the adventures which befell a civil servant tired of his office job.

From the Evening Chronicle 16 July, 1953.

4

This is the weather the cuckoo likes,
And so do I;
When showers betumble the chestnut spikes,
And nestlings fly ...

Weathers, Thomas Hardy

For a moment James was totally confused then he realised what had happened. The great jib had turned like a weather vane in the changing wind as, when not in use, the crane was left to swing free. Otherwise, blowing with full force on the side of the crane, a gale would topple it over. He looked round the yard and down the Tyne. Every single crane faced the same direction.

Meanwhile the kestrel hadn't moved, though the wind whistling through her wire nest sounded like a steam train. For most of the day the gale blew while James huddled behind the cabin, fearing for his life. The male kestrel had not returned that day, unable to ride the fierce winds raging between the girders, and the sitting bird was now showing signs of uneasiness.

Suddenly the wind dropped and James quickly took the opportunity to hurriedly, but with great care, descend the one hundred and forty rungs, counting each one as he went and hoping the winds would not return until he was at the bottom. Whilst he had been used to some dangerous and risky situations photographing and drawing wildlife, nothing had prepared him for this.

On the following day he returned and all seemed as normal, the shipyard operating with its busy, noisy, daily work and the kestrels resuming their daily chores.

Four weeks later, five of the eggs had hatched successfully. The remaining one was ejected from the nest after a few more days since it was showing no signs of development. This was not an act of cruelty as, instinctively, the kestrel knew that all eggs had to be hatched at around the same time for maximum survival rate of the chicks. The nestlings were all like powder puffs, with their proud mother keeping them warm and showing a surprising tenderness.

Every so often the male kestrel called from a short distance away, and the female, brooding her restless down-covered chicks, replied with a higher pitched call. It was a conversation telling her that dinner had arrived, and leaving the nest, she retrieved the mouse he had brought, clutching it in her strong talons. Each chick was fed individually with a small morsel, she only fed herself on the coarse or bony bits.

Now, the working crane swung round and the nest caught the hot midday sun. Quickly she dropped her wings and straddled the chicks as they jostled and pushed for a place in the shade. She gasped and panted in the heat. But all was well, and the nestlings grew strong, their rust and brown feathers peeping through their baby down.

By now, they had learned to grasp the wire strands of the nest with their sharp claws as they exercised their growing wings and played a sort of game of tag along the girders, panicking if they lost their balance and rushing back to the safety of the nest to recover.

Preening was now essential to remove the irksome down and, as if to exercise their eyes that would soon spot a mouse

at two hundred feet
from up in the sky, they
watched the
downy feathers
falling
in the
air
currents
about the
girders.

Then
came the day when the parents
would not return to the nest, instead calling from a nearby
crane. The first youngster launched itself into the vastness
below, dropping and teetering uncertainly on the air, then,
with frantic winnowing and ruddering, triumphantly
controlling its flight to circle and land next to the parents.

The second eldest sat on the girder contemplating the
plunge he would soon have to make, the others looked
somewhat glum, and might wait a little longer.

And that was the photographer's last view of the kestrel
family on the crane, as they were all about to fly. It was time
for him to dismantle the camera and the hide, so he did not
witness one of the youngsters misjudge the wind as he
desperately tried to master his flying instincts. A sudden gust
took him by surprise and sent him into an uncontrollable spin,
plunging downwards toward the distant ground below. The
next time the photographer saw this young kestrel it would be
at closer quarters.

5

I will not be clapped in a hood,
Nor a cage, or alight upon wrist,
Now I have learnt to be proud
Hovering over the wood
In the broken mist
Or tumbling cloud.

The Hawk, William Butler Yeats

The baby kestrel looked the picture of misery. He sat with his head hunched between his shoulders, eyes dull and with good reason. On his first flight he had landed in a bucket of bilge oil, unable to flap a wing until a passing worker rescued him and took him to the yard's first aid centre, where he was kept in a large cardboard box.

'Why, he was savage. He'd hev taken me hand off if aa hadn't thrown something ower him.'

Here, where they handled with tenderness and skill the accidents of a hazardous occupation, where the removal of a steel splinter, the soothing of a bad burn, the setting of a broken toe, was a daily occurrence, the little falcon presented a problem. How to help a creature whose plumage was a black, gritty, coagulated mass? They sent for James, who took him away in his box.

The kestrel was taken home, where a little olive oil was carefully poured over him, and he was handled very carefully. His feet were bound in rags – while he couldn't quite take a hand off, he could still inflict a nasty scratch. The oil was gently worked into his feathers to reduce the heavy, sticky, mineral oil and the black ooze gently squeezed out with cotton wool. Meanwhile, a warm soapy bath was prepared for him. His head was now wrapped in cloth, then his body was immersed and washed in repeated changes of water until his rust coloured plumage began to show. Then his feet were unwrapped and each one was gently scrubbed with a soft nail brush. Now his whole body was wrapped in a dry cloth, his head-covering was removed and his head cleansed in the same manner. Finally he was dabbed all over with dry towels, not rubbed, for that would have broken his feathers, and put into a warm place in a lidless box. Although he was now clean again he was a sorry sight indeed, with his scrawny neck and breastbone protruding sharply through his wet spiky feathers.

Two hours later, he was transformed. His feathers had dried – he had helped the drying by shaking himself like a dog and raising the feathers – and his eyes had regained their eager sparkle. He was hungry too!

James came and, looking down at him, talked to him gently. The bird glared malevolently back. He'd received some rough treatment from this creature in the last few hours.

A hand reached into the box to touch him and he hurled himself back, panting and hissing passionately, with his beak open. The hand came nearer and he lashed out with cat-like speed to dig his talons into the fingers, and gripped.

The photographer winced, but made no attempt to withdraw his hand. Instead, he pushed it nearer, against the back of the other foot so that the kestrel had to step onto the hand or overbalance. Having little choice, he gripped the hand with his other foot as well, was lifted out of the box, and James sat with him quietly until he regained his composure. He relaxed his grip and stretched his yellow toes out across the fingers. This hand was now not a hand; it was a perch.

He watched another hand reach out to pick up a piece of red, raw, pigeon meat, with feather still attached, to dangle this invitingly before him. He braced himself suspiciously but hunger gnawed at his innards, and he could not resist the temptation. Twenty-four hours earlier he had refused the offer of bread and cheese from a kindly but bird-ignorant workman. Now at last he could see red raw flesh. The meat waggled enticingly nearer. With a quick sideways motion of his head he reached out and snatched it from the fingers and swallowed it, feathers and all, in a greedy gulp.

More tender morsels were offered, and each one was taken with lessening suspicion until finally he was offered a white-feathered leg, which he clutched possessively to his breast before leaping with it to a table top to tear at it rapaciously.

Now he felt comfortable, full. His feathers, which were still growing, itched, and he shook himself vigorously to rid himself of dandruff-like pieces of scale and broken baby down. The mineral oil and soapy bath had removed every trace of natural oil from his plumage and it was soft and lifeless as he ran his hooked bill down his mantle.

He raised his lower eyelids which gave him a mild sleepy look and he began to preen. The hooked, blue beak seemed quite unsuitable for this operation, but one swift sure stroke from base to tip down the quill of each primary closed the ragged-looking gaps in the vane. Each flat vane, which would provide the thrust in flight, was really made up of thousands of minute interlocking hooks, which, if they were broken apart, could easily be snapped shut by the preening action.

The wing and tail quills were treated in this fashion and then the bird rubbed the side of his beak and face in his oil gland which was situated at the base of his tail, and wiped a thin film of this oil on the preened feathers. In this way, stroking, nibbling, and wiping, he went over all of his plumage until he had some semblance of his former beauty. It would take many such preenings before his feathers were properly oiled, but he was satisfied for now. He was warm, dry, and his crop bulged comfortably. He tucked his head into his mantle and slept.

While he slept a jess was prepared for him. This was a leather thong, about eight inches long, double slotted at one end. The slotted end would be passed around his leg and the free end threaded through the slots to form a non-slip noose. This jess would be used to leash him to his perch, and to control him while on the hand.

A foot high wooden log was obtained, and a staple driven into its flat top. This, known to the falconer as the block, was placed in the centre of a sanded tray, and all was ready for the kestrel's waking.

He hated the leather jess at first. When he was fastened to his block he tugged at the leather thong with his leg extended, beating his wings and kekking shrilly. After a short while he leapt onto the block and sat sullenly, with his head between his shoulders, retiring behind his hate. Soon he began to preen once more. James decided to give the bird a name: Kek.

An hour later Kek began to preen once more. The sanded tray was littered with his first white faeces, for his metabolic rate was high, and soon he began to feel the effects of his tussle with the jess, and the effort of preening, in hunger.

A white feathered pigeon leg appeared before him and he weakened. His wings drooped slightly and he gave them a half beat, but sat where he was on the centre of the block. A hand reached out with a tender piece of raw flesh between the fingers and he snatched this. A second piece was offered, just out of reach so that he had to take a step forward to get it. A third piece appeared, a foot away from the edge of the block. To get this he would have to step onto the other hand which was placed next to the block.

He hesitated; the hands were steady; the red meat was so inviting. He hopped forward to the full extent of his leash and gave up his independence. For the time being at least.

Eventually, with regular feeding, the kestrel became accustomed to his new environment, but James knew that the bird had to be taught to catch his own prey to be able to survive on his own in the wild. Several weeks of patient training now followed with gentle yet firm commands, rewarded with tasty meals. Kek quickly learned to fly from his block to James's wrist for titbits, and return on command 'to your perch'.

By now his wings and tail had grown full length and he had preened away the last vestiges of baby down. He had also had his first bath in a tray in the garden.

When James had fetched a bucket of water he had splashed it with his hand before pouring it into the tray. The sound and sight of the splashing water produced a strange reaction in Kek who leapt to the grass, and, fluffing out his breast and flank feathers and drooping his wings, had pressed himself to the ground and wriggled and dipped in an ecstacy of false bathing. When the water was poured into the tray he leapt into it and pushed his head and beak into the hand that playfully splashed water over him.

Until now his flights out-of-doors had been quite short and he had been untethered only when he was hungry. It was only his hunger and training which kept him from a sudden dash for freedom.

It was in the evening, just after his feed, that he made his first escape. The retaining slot at one end of the jess had worn, and one of his powerful bursts of wing beating broke the thong. Suddenly he found himself air-borne, fully fed, and uncommanded. James came out into the garden just in time to see him sailing over the house tops, a fan-tailed silhouette against the golden evening sky.

James was out and about at sunrise, and almost the first bird he picked up though his binoculars was Kek, floating high in the clear morning air, his underparts aglow from the rays of the rising sun, his jess trailing from a leg. About him swooped a band of twittering swallows whose playful dives he avoided with an expert flick of the wings. Kek tried to hover repeatedly, but even his vibrating wing tips couldn't hold him in his airy seat and he stalled and slid to a new pitch. Perhaps it was the swallows that unbalanced him, but the man couldn't help thinking that Kek's inborn ability to hover needed practice to perfect it.

The kestrel slid into a long glide that lost height quickly. Half a mile later he braked and landed on the very tip of the jib of a small crane which was poised on the edge of a quarry. James panted after him, approached the crane, and spoke his name quietly.

Kek looked down curiously. That sound 'Kek' was associated with food, and right now he was hungry. The man climbed the steel ladder up the side of the engine house, onto the roof, then gingerly began to crawl up the jib. A piece of red meat and feathers fluttered in his hand, and Kek's feelings of hunger and fear clashed. The hand reached out for the dangling jess and, just at the moment that distrust won and his wings opened for flight, the fingers gripped the leash and held.

Bating and screaming he was fastened to a wrist and carried to the ground, and back to his block. There he sulked for an hour until hunger made him fly to his capturer for food.

Meanwhile, as happens with all young kestrels, his brothers and sisters had been on many flights with their parents. At first food was brought to them as they sat on their high perches on the cranes. Later, following their parents on expeditions along the river, they copied their hunting techniques. In comparison Kek had much to learn.

His training continued throughout the autumn. Flights from the block were extended until he could fly at the sound of a whistle from two hundred yards away. Then came the moment of triumph when, with a pigeon's breast clutched in his talons, a whole meal that was the key to his freedom, he launched from the wrist at the command 'to your perch'. Trees fringed the field invitingly. Would he resist their call? Would his training hold? The answer came as, sailing fast downwind, he shot past the block, wheeled, and beat up slowly to settle gently upon it.

For the rest of the winter, until the sparrows began to pick the leaves from the yellow crocuses in spring, he practised hunting with a rubber mouse. This decoy had a length of nylon attached to its head and was jerked through the grass below the kestrel's perch. Eventually he could catch the mouse with lightning speed whichever way it was pulled.

Indoors, his food was thrown at him as he sat on his block, and he learned to catch it with a slash of his talons. At the word 'catch' he would poise himself like a thunderbolt, his eyes ablaze. If the food was thrown above him he would hurl himself up in a somersault to catch it in both talons, then right himself with a flip of a wing.

Autumn gales had stripped the last leaves from the trees about the open common where Kek was exercised, and a strong wind was blowing as he beat upwing ready to land on his block. Just as he was about to settle, a blustering wind rose under his fanned tail sending him upwards, and he found himself floating high. A new excitement gripped him. Oblivious to whistle and waving lure, he angled across wind and was lost to sight.

Days passed, until, exactly a week later, James was driving near the scene of Kek's escape. Straight up the road towards him flew a flock of starlings, and behind them in hot pursuit, was a familiar winnowing figure. The starlings sped over a wall towards some trees and disappeared with the swooping kestrel close behind. Thrilled at the sight, James leapt from his car, clambered up the wall and began to whistle shrilly, much to the astonishment of a man out walking his dog. Kek had swooped and missed, and was slashing at wind-blown leaves in anger.

Hearing the whistling he turned and stared, then rose and flew into the branches of a tree. James dropped to the ground and walked quietly up to him calling him by name the while. 'Hello Kek. So you've turned up again, Kek.' Meanwhile he fumbled through his pockets for something to use as a lure, an odd feather perhaps ... and Kek was once more in his possession.

The crocuses died, and the sparrows began to squabble over pigeon feathers that littered the lawn around Kek's block. New feathers had appeared on the kestrel's crown and nape which had a distinct grey tinge, and others in bis mantle were clean and bright, almost pinkish, compared to his first juvenile plumage. He had also replaced two lost feathers in his tail but, except for abrasion round their edges, his primaries were untouched. A falcon's moult is a gradual process, for flight is his living. He cannot, like a blackbird, go into hiding in the shrubbery while he grows new flight and tail feathers.

At this time, James had bought a hamster for his children and when it first emerged from its box in a wire cage, the kestrel was surprised to say the least. Rodents are the food of kestrels but the hamster did not know this and they eyed each other through the bars, nose to beak.

Now the swallows had returned and were idling above in a warm sky when a black cat appeared among the blackcurrant bushes, her eyes ablaze with desire for this strange bird that sat so still upon the block. She made a crouching but tentative run across the lawn, for her instinct warned that this was no ordinary bird. Kek yickered in fear and bated powerfully from the block. The black cat ran ungracefully back into the bushes while the kestrel beat his wings and clawed at the ground with his free leg.

The jess, which he had been working on continuously for days ('I must replace it with a new one,' James had said) snapped, and he hurtled into flight, gave a triple 'kek, kek, kek' that echoed shrilly from the house tops, and disappeared into the blue.

Every adventure that Kek would encounter from then on could only be imagined by the photographer, but he was confident that the kestrel he had cared for so long now had the skills to survive. The following chapters simply tell the story of what *might* have happened to Kek.

6

And above, in the light
Of the star-lit night,
Swift birds of passage wing their flight.

Birds of Passage, Henry Wadsworth Longfellow

Kek spent his first night of freedom on a great pylon. In the morning he was ravenous and he was soon foraging over the dewy fields, but without success. He descended onto the end of a large barn where he scared a half-dozen crooning pigeons which clattered away but soon returned to sit on the other end of the building. In some instinctive way they knew that he was no pigeon killer.

From his perch he overlooked an untidy stack yard about which swooped twittering swallows, and from a little fir coppice at the end of the yard he could hear a willow warbler singing his pretty, but somehow sad, descending-scale song with its curious upwind inflections at the end. A group of noisy sparrows squabbled about a muddy tractor. Five cocksparrows, with flattened bodies, drooped wings and spread, elevated, tails were directing their garrulous display at a single dowdy hen, who took refuge among the tractor's wheels.

Kek's eyes fired at the sight. Their movements resembled the jerkings of the rubber mouse. He hurled himself down in a silent glide amidst the passerine scrimmage, hardly paused as his yellow talon dropped to grapple the unwary unfortunate cock that was singled out, and swooped up into a haystack.

The sparrows and the swallows scattered, and the stack yard became silent for a while. But only for a while! One sparrow's death would not dam the song which the tiny willow warbler had flown two thousand miles to sing, nor stop the swallow from adding pellets of mud to his nest in the cow-byre.

Refreshed and stimulated by his first real kill, Kek spiralled up on the high west wind and drifted across country to a large dark wood, two miles distant, in which he could see the glint of a lake. Four minutes later he glided down and settled in a pine top in the bird sanctuary.

The sanctuary was maintained by a local ornithological society and, although it was almost surrounded by the bricks and mortar of housing estates, a keen watcher could still show an exciting list of birds. No keener watcher existed than Kek, who made the sanctuary his home for three months and saw the passage of birds, the sight of which would have started many a heated discourse on rarities among the society's members.

He saw the secret arrival of 'difficult' warblers that furtively haunted the reed beds about the lake for a day before disappearing northwards, and saw the black and yellow flash of a cock golden oriole which many a watcher would have given his telescope to see. He noted

JA

the arrival of the osprey, who created a great stir among the
lake's waterfowl as he sailed on his broad pinions a hundred
feet above the lake. He watched the fowl scurry to the reeds'
shelter or dive with protesting quack as the grey bird of
prey circled, staggered and dropped vertically, his wings
trailing above him, his thick white thighs and scuted
legs with their terminating grapnels reaching
below. The osprey struck the water with a
great splash, and seconds later rose in a
shower of foam with a huge, struggling
perch impaled on his
     talons.

JA

He swung upwards and almost
immediately gripped the fish
with one foot behind the other
so that it was pointed head first into the wind,
to cut down drag. He flew with it into the dark wood, but was
disturbed there and circled overhead, on one occasion
breaking away to soar over the nearby estate. Not one pair of
eyes was raised to observe that wondrous and rare sight
above.

The sanctuary and its immediate fields throbbed with new
life: life that was inextricably linked with death. Caterpillars
were thrust into the hungry gapes of small birds. Before the
larvae had wriggled their last, the nestlings were plucked from
their beds by beady eyed jays to be fed to their own raucous
young. Some lives never got beyond a pulse in an egg. Others
grew into pretty little things that were slaughtered as they

prepared to take their first step. The warbler and the
blackbird, the jaunty wren and blue winged jay, the shrill
voiced shrew and persistent weasel, none was innocent of
killing. The caterpillar that chewed the leaf, and the wood
pigeon that swallowed the sweet corn, all destroyed life to
live.

And among them, Kek was not slow to learn. The green,
growing corn and lush pastures were alive with mice and
voles. From his pitch above, looking down the vertical stems
of corn, he could watch the comings and goings of every tiny
creature that appeared at the mouth of earthen tunnel or
grassy run. Field mouse and vole, tiny shrew fighting with
relatively huge worm, plump water vole contentedly nibbling
water plants by the ditch, all had heard the hiss of his wings
and felt his needle talons. Even the velvet furred mole, pushing
his little hillock upwards with pink nose, had been torn from
his tunnel. Nor were the choicer things that crawled disdained.
Fat larvae and glossy beetles harmful to the farmer's corn were
swallowed whole.

And as he became fitter, he daily tore savagely at the jess
with his strong hooked beak, a little piece at a time. Snap, his
beak would sound
as the hard
mandibles clicked
off the leather fibres.
Snap, snap, until a
final tug jerked free
his symbol of
captivity, and he
dropped it below
into a ditch.

When midsummer passed, Kek felt an urge to explore the countryside to the east where he could see a huge grey pit heap. The heap was burning slowly and its reek greatly annoyed the residents of the estate to the south when the wind blew in that direction. Perched on the tip of the trolley rails at its summit, he surveyed the countryside about him.

It was almost flat for miles around, with only a few undulations. Encircling the east, six miles away, was the thin cold blue of the North Sea. To the north, beyond pit villages and small townships were the lovely Cheviots. Smog from the city obscured the beautiful moorlands to the west and an almost unbroken sea of roof tops stretched down to the smoke shrouded Tyne almost three miles to the south.

He could see the jibs of the cranes and derricks towering from the valley, and he felt strangely stirred at this.

A muddy lane meandered through the grimy cornfields about the pit heap, on one side of it was a smelly rubbish dump, and on the other a rushy pond which had been formed many years before by subsidence and flooding of the Rising Sun pit. Waterhens, snipe and reed bunting haunted it, as well as puffy cheeked water voles and brown rats. It was grand hunting country. It was possible, indeed, to hunt without flying or hovering, for lines of power pylons cut across the fields. Perched on the high cables he had an unrestricted view of the ground below and he had only to move along a few yards to survey a new beat. Other kestrels hunted the area too, perhaps his own family, but he would never have recognised them

Rosebay willow herb grew in profusion by the cindery lane, brightening its dinginess with their rosy spikes, when the first dunlin arrived at the pond. They had flown all night, and swung through the early morning mists to land on the pond's muddy edge. The near stagnant water was rich in the larvae of mosquito which hung from its still surface, and the dunlin busied themselves refuelling on these, oblivious to the bird watcher a few yards away. They were eight in number and in form were typical of the wader tribe, with their boat shaped bodies, long slender bills for probing, long legs for wading and pointed

Dunlin

JA

powerful wings for fast flying. All save one were either juveniles or adults which had already acquired winter plumage, and the odd one still had the rich chestnut and blade upperparts, and black belly of the breeding season. When they had eaten sufficiently, they retired in a little group to a clump of rush roots that protruded above the water, tucked their beaks below their mantles, and slept. Two boys paddled nearby on a home-made raft of oil drums and pallets, for this was also a playground for the local lads.

They had been joined meanwhile by a pair of redshanks, cautious, almost neurotic birds that waded quickly in the shallows, picking here and there, stopping to bob their rear ends with a peculiar backward jerk of their heads whenever they thought they saw something suspicious, and flying off to the other end of the pond with an explosive 'teen-teen' of alarm, presently to repeat the performance in the other direction.

Three ruffs flew in, or at least, two ruffs and a reeve. Big, silent birds that busied themselves feeding, disappearing and reappearing among the clumps of rushes, the ruffs being distinctly bigger than the reeve. It was a pity, the bird watcher mused, that the cocks had lost their gorgeous Elizabethan ruffs and ear tufts of spring. Then, on a northern tundra, those very same birds had spread wide their ruffs, one a rich chestnut, the other ringed with black and white,

for hardly two birds were ruffed alike, and had fought fiercely for the favours of the demure hen. Now, ruffless and virtually sexless, they fed quietly side by side.

Throughout August and into September, unusual and rare birds stopped at the stagnant pond, sometimes for days on end. This was a refuelling point where they transformed food into muscle and fat, stored energy that would be burned up on long night flights. Wood and green sandpiper, newly down from Scandinavian forests, might be seen feeding about the pools at the base of the rubbish dump, a strange contrast of grace and beauty with ugliness and stench. The little stint, like a diminutive dunlin, fed with those birds, and the dark, white rumped greenshank, which may have bred in the Cairngorms, waded taller and more graceful still than the redshank.

Recently arrived from Russia, a marsh sandpiper, like a little greenshank, caused great argument among the birdwatchers until its identity was finally fixed, and, like an escapee from some cartoonist's sketch book, a black winged stilt paid a fleeting visit to the pond. Although its body was not as bulky as the greenshanks, its legs were twice as long and trailed behind it in flight like a piece of rope.

All these lovely birds and more, visited the unsightly spot which would one day soon lose its value to them. The towns would continue to spew their filth, the waggons would continue to articulate with their loads, the great caterpillar tractors would level all, and finally, a sign would rise saying 'Valuable land for sale'. But there was still hope!

The lower flowers of the willow herb spires seeded, and were replaced with white, curling fibres that would float in the breeze with their seeds to explore and sow other wastes, and children satisfied their harvesting instincts by plucking grimy blackberries from tangles by the laneside. Summer had long flown south with the last wheatears which had hopped through the sharp golden stubble. Now flocks of fierce eyed gulls squabbled with rooks and crows on the edge of the rubbish dump, or floated serenely on the pond's surface, littering it with white feathers that sailed like little Nile boats in the breeze to accumulate as a white tide line on the muddy shore. Among them was a huge glaucous gull, white like the Arctic ice he had flown in from. His back was the palest of blue-grey, like morning mist, and his red spotted yellow beak was cruel, his little eye avaricious.

Cheerful bands of linnets and greenfinches tilted from stubble to briar, and noisy flocks of spangled starlings foraged with lapwings between tip and pond.

Hunting was still good for Kek, but a restlessness urged him to extend his range. One day, he brought up a casting that contained the bones and fur of two field voles and dropping it down the pit heap, he launched himself into a long glide which he maintained by occasional winnowing wind beats.

Three miles later, the ground steeped away from him suddenly and the giant crane loomed before him. He circled it once then swooped among its girders and settled. Two hundred feet below, the muddy Tyne swirled. Kek was home again.

He settled into the dockland hunting routine as if he had received training from his parents. Instinctively he knew the right places. The muddy beaches at low tide; the weed grown banks behind warehouses and sheds: the tired looking fields that pushed almost to the river side.

Down river, on its south side, he discovered Jarrow Slake, a huge tidal mud flat. Thousands of golden plover, curlew, redshank and dunlin fed on the ooze and, as the tide crept in, retreated before it to the safety of a little island on its inner edge, where they slept. On the western bank of the Slake, next to a slow running river, the Don, a tributary of the Tyne, stands the pride of Jarrow, the Venerable Bede's ancient Saxon church. In the time of that great scholar, the Slake must have been a great fen where wild fowl and waders, now rarities, bred commonly.

As the centuries passed, and the Tyne was improved, the birds continued to come, but not to breed. Instead they used the Slake as a refuelling point for their long migratory flights or, if they had reached a southerly enough point, wintered there.

But for how long? Reclamation, the death-knell of wild fowl, had been discussed in the local papers.

All this meant nothing to Kek. His little brain merely registered the fact that the Slake's untidy, weedy banks were a good hunting ground. Even had he the intelligence to think about it, his first thought might have been, 'I should worry? My kind nested in trees and cliffs, then in man's ruins, and now in the heart of his kingdom. We still survive.'

He continued to roost on the crane in a sheltered angle, and his castings accumulated on the steel ledge, little coffins that contained the broken skeletons of his prey. The days were shorter now and his hunting was more concentrated.

Each evening, as he settled down to roost, he was increasingly disturbed by the arrival of lusty, dusky, spangled birds that flew in wavering aerial displays about the giant before settling down among the girders, where they chirruped and whistled like riotous boys before going to sleep. They were continental starlings, arriving in waves from the Baltic coasts and Russia.

And then one evening it happened. So far their numbers had been relatively small and they kept a respectful distance from his roosting ledge. On this evening, in November, they arrived in black waves that joined forces and swept, first with a hiss then a roar of wings, about the crane. They commanded the evening sky and amazed the workmen below. A murmuration of starlings? A Niagara Falls of starlings, a tempest of starlings might be a better term.

They fell upon the giant and massed upon every ledge and

girder, shuffling and re-shuffling, shoulder to shoulder, until they even invaded the sanctity of Kek's ledge and he cringed back in fear. The air was filled with an unbelievable sound, their droppings pattered like rain and oozed white down the steelwork. The temperature rose many degrees from the heat of their multitudinous bodies and a musky stench pervaded all.

Distressed and insulted by the excreta that marked his plumage, Kek dropped out of the jib and flew along to No. 8 where he roosted on a fishplate below the engine house. The wire nest was still there, rusty and silent.

The starling invasion caused consternation to the humans too. Permission was given to the men to shoot them in an attempt to scare them off and guns were fired point blank among them. Great numbers were killed and many were maimed, but it was like trying to draw the ocean away with a ladle. Perhaps fifty thousand of their kind roosted each night in the reed bed in the sanctuary five miles away. And each night, as they circled over the lake in their last fling before bedding down, on the cranes they were waited on below by the menacing forms of three sparrow hawks, which took their toll with deadly certainty. The starlings could see the hawks and

knew their purpose, but still came to roost in the reed bed.

Cold winds now soughed through the girders at night and on some mornings the rough banks behind the yard were hoary with frost. Mice, shrews and voles were harder to find now, for great numbers of the adults that had bred that year had died off, leaving their vigorous young to survive the coming winter. Kek occasionally took toll of the sparrows as they fed on crumbs thrown by workers, but on the whole they were wily birds and retreated nimbly into the shelter of the great sheds as his silhouette appeared above.

All of the migratory birds that preferred warmer weather had long since flown south, but not quite all of them. A schoolboy was birdspotting by the banks of the Slake, and almost the first bird he saw was a wheatear, blown off course from North Africa or beyond.

It stayed well into December and was eventually trapped and examined, and a little numbered ring encircled its leg when it was released. What strange urge had driven it from hot Arabian deserts, northwards to Britain in winter the watchers asked. How could it, a purely insectivorous bird, hope to survive the bitter conditions that fast approached?

Two days later the ground was icebound and a sleet laden wind whined through the square tower of the Saxon church. Kek sat on one corner, hunched and empty-cropped, for two hours of diligent search and three stoops at sparrows had been abortive.

Out of sight below him, the little wheatear, fast weakening,

Desert Wheatear   James Alder

searched for spiders under the eroded banks of the Slake. It fluttered from bankside and hopped aimlessly among frozen stones and lime-encrusted bricks that littered the shore, then listlessly examined the rim of a worn-smooth motor tyre. Snowflakes touched plumage that was designed to blend with hot sandy wastes.

A few moments later it was limp and crushed as Kek landed again on the old church tower. The bitter wind sighed through the ancient windows as he crouched and tore at the still warm bird.

That night Kek roosted on an oak beam in the tower.

R Alder

7

Blow, blow, thou winter wind
Thou art not so unkind …
As You Like It, William Shakespeare

By now, Kek had replaced most of his first flight and tail feathers with new ones. His tail was a mixture of old, worn, barred feathers and new greyish ones with slight incomplete bars. His body feathers had been completely changed, his mantle being pinker with dark inverted arrow-shaped marks and his head had a grey tinge, while his breast was a fine creamy buff with dark brown drop-shaped and arrow markings.

Evolution had designed him as the perfect flyer. Although he was normally leisurely in his cross-country flying, he could develop a great turn of speed at will, with fast manoeuvring and, of course, his hovering was a delight to watch. Strangely, he rarely attempted to pursue birds in full flight although he might have caught them easily, but instead stooped at them as they fed or perched. He was so organized to catch his quarry in the downward rush that it never occurred to him to harry it if he missed, but gave up after a short chase.

The strains of Christmas carols rose up into the old square tower when Kek felt urged to fly over the wide, plover strewn Slake, over a shipyard strange to him, down river with the yellow, swirling flood. Tanker and tramp, liner and launch, lay hull to hull below him. Coaling stations, dry docks and tubby, chuggy, fishing boats slid below until he flew over gull lined

Lloyd's jetty with its hailing station, where the comings and goings of the world's ships were recorded. Here, river met sea to form a great bay which was almost enclosed by the concrete prongs of North and South piers.

Black cormorants fished or sat upon buoys with their wings extended in the breeze and gulls and kittiwakes paddled gracefully in line along the oily effluence from two stinking sewers, awaiting the dainty morsels which would eddy to the surface.

Above an eroded cliff on the north side, a huge statue of Lord Collingwood, who had fought with Nelson, stared stonily out over the bay. Kek floated down to scare away four disrespectful pigeons, and settled upon his white head.

To his left were the remains of an old castle dominating a cliff top, and a beautiful priory. Across the river a Roman station had been discovered. The place breathed history. It had atmosphere, albeit a slightly grimy one.

Extending his wings he dropped slightly into the breeze and, still without a wing beat, felt for the updraught of air from the cliff face. Finding it, he angled along the grassy cliff top, the automatic pilot at his nerve centre making all the split second decisions that maintained lift and height. He stopped, facing the breeze almost horizontally, and quite still for the strong up-currents gave him all the lift necessary. One leg dangled like a pendulum below him and he swung this to and fro to shift his centre of gravity as the air current varied in its strength. Nothing moved below so he tilted on one wing to slide sideways to a new pitch, stopped, and watched.

A pair of tiny shrews fought below a tangle of thistles. They always fought if they met each other as fighting and eating were their livelihood. Usually the fighting ended with the victor eating the vanquished, for their metabolic rate was so high that they ate everything they could kill, and consumed at least their own weight in food every day. They didn't even sleep properly at night, but went on hunting in fits and starts lest in a long sleep they died of starvation. For this reason they couldn't hibernate through the winter.

They tumbled and squeaked in high pitched voices that were almost beyond human hearing, trying to find a vital spot with their sharp teeth, and one fell from out of the thistle cover. He never rejoined in battle, but felt instead the momentary crush of cruel talons.

Kek sat upon Collingwood's shoulder, protected from the cold wind by his head, and scratched his ear coverts with a knobbled foot. His crop was comfortably full: at least two hours of energy were contained in the ten grams of shrew, all of which he had eaten, feet, tail and all. The harbour had nice hunting possibilities.

Below him a dusky rock pipit ran along the cliff top, urgently picking here and there. Its diet was a varied one of insects and small creatures left on the rocks by the outflowing tide, as well as seeds, and it was able to endure the hardest of weathers. Dissatisfied by its cliff top foraging, it gave a 'tseep, tseep' and launched itself into space with the intention of flying down to the black rocks below.

From below a meteoric blue shape, sickle winged, rose to meet it, and the pipit towered in panicky flight on the strong updraught. The little cock merlin, with magnificent strategy, pushed the frightened pipit higher, then with a tremendous burst of power flung himself at it.

The pipit feinted and the merlin missed, his impetuous rush carrying him fifty feet above it. Wheeling, he stooped with all his power, and again the pipit, wings straining to their limit, feinted to the right and doubled back and the little falcon chattered his chagrin. This time his stoop had such power that by the time he wheeled to attack again, the pipit, choosing its moment to perfection, dropped like a stone to a ditch on the cliff top, with the merlin plummeting behind.

The excitement was too much for Kek, who flung himself off Collingwood in a powered dive and pursued the unwitting merlin downwards.

In the ensuing scrimmage the pipit escaped below an overhanging tussock, and Kek and the merlin spiralled up and out from the cliff over the bay, their shrill chattering voices ringing out angrily. Kek was bulkier than the merlin, but hadn't his speed and he was soon left behind in the playful chase that followed. The merlin sped low across the bay and over the south pier. Kek returned to the statue, where he preened and oiled his feathers. An hour later he was hunting again and this time this time caught a mouse in bankside allotments above the hailing station.

For two days he profitably hunted the bay, roosting at night in a comfortable niche in the cliff face below Collingwood, before he felt the wanderlust again. He left the statue behind, flew over the priory and the castle and turned north into a bitter wind that had a hint of snow. A heavy grey sea thundered across barren yellow sand which was useless for hunting, so he sidled inland to follow a coastal electric railway with its weedy embankments. Two miles of fruitless hunting followed until he climbed over the seaside holiday resort with its empty boarding houses, and saw the wide links beyond

that stretched down to steep banks and thence to the sand. This was more to his liking. By now his crop craved food.

North of the town, below a miniature golf course, the bank to the sea was untidy and muddy. Little rivulets gashed the bank and washed yellow mud across the sand to join the incoming tide. In many places the waterlogged bank top had fallen away in large lumps which the sea would soon pound to pieces. Wherever man relaxed, the sea tried to reclaim.

Beside one of these muddy rivulets a buck rat fed on a washed up fish. There was nothing loathsome about him. He was big and strong, bright of eye and finely furred: seaside living did him well, and he was ready to accept almost anything that the sea cared to offer.

Kek slid over the bank and saw him instantly. He flexed his wings and dived, bringing his talons forward in a smooth swinging movement, ready to grapple.

Not for nothing had the buck reached his third winter. His instinct spoke of danger long before Kek reached him. Had he run, he would certainly have died, but instead he backed against the stinking fish, his great yellow incisor teeth bared in a horrific grimace. Kek was unnerved at the last split second and swung to one side, then climbed away, defeated.

The sand gave way to a rocky shore, and beyond a headland through flurries of snow and sleet he could see a lighthouse, standing cold and invincible on a tidal island. Rough fields stretched inland from a wave pounded clay bank, here only twenty or so feet high, but around the headland the grey seas thundered across a wide bay to crash against the foot of a beetling cliff. Bladderwrack and throng weed, torn up from the sea bed by turbulent currents had piled up in a deep brown wall along the tideline and tortoiseshell coloured

turnstones ran along it searching for small creatures, now and then leaping nervously as each incoming wave heaved the slippery mass.

Instinctively, Kek knew this to be a good kestrel country and he angled down to rest on a telegraph post that carried the line to the lighthouse. To keep a footing, he had to streamline his body into the wind and dig his talons into the wood. He sat there morosely for a while, eyeing the ground hungrily, flicking his nictating membrane – his third eyelid – across his eye occasionally to wipe off the lashing sleet.

JA

Presently he opened his wings, released his grip, and the hissing wind carried him effortlessly up and backwards so that he had quickly to readjust his centre of gravity and fling his weight forwards. Head down, as a man might against the wind, he progressed slowly without a wingbeat, but rising and falling, teetering to this side and that until he reached out with his talons and grabbed the top of the next post.

Below him, snow had piled up against the windward side of the tussocky grass. Under one of these tussocks, which curved over him with the wind, a hare had made a cosy form and was nibbling some of his own droppings. This was not unnatural, but a habit essential to his wellbeing.

Kek saw the movement of his soft nose and gave a hungry start but checked himself as he realised that this was no small creature. But something had to turn up. That nag inside of him had to be satisfied.

His left eye registered a tiny movement over his shoulder and his whole head swivelled round to focus both eyes on the spot. The mouse had flicked out of sight into his tunnel. Kek continued to stare.

A trembling pointed nose and two bright beady eyes appeared at the tunnel. Kek tensed. The whole mouse appeared, and sat up to pull at a head of grass seed.

He never knew what hit him. Kek, landing across wind in a difficult pounce, was bowled over as he hit the tussock. But he had the mouse clenched in his foot when he lifted in the wind. It was definitely a fine catch.

That night he roosted in a niche between bales of straw on the lee side of a stack in the corner of a field. Peewits huddled in the stubble and partridges 'jugged' together in a circle, their heralds facing outwards. All night long the wind whined, intermittently laden with sleet and snow, and the sea moaned and the surf hissed across the rocky foreshore. It seemed incredible that warm blooded creatures could exist in the open under such conditions, but their temperature was much

higher than man's. As long as they were well fed their remarkable insulating layers of feathers would maintain their blood heat.

In the morning the landscape was forbidding. Wet, grey snow clung in crusty layers to the windward side of post, wall, tussock and stack, etching the uncovered lee side in harsh contrast. The peewits had flown to the tide line, and where the partridge jugged was a circle in the snow, kept clear by the heat of their bodies, and within it, a concentric ring of their droppings.

Kek began his hunting early and instinctively took his pitch at fifty feet above the tussocky field where he had killed the fieldmouse. He was not the only hunter out early. Below him appeared a big buff coloured bird with long coloured wings, which it beat slowly and silently in sweeping arcs. Its flight was rolling, easy, and occasionally it hesitated and hovered, not as skilfully as Kek, but well enough. This was a short eared owl, who had drifted in from Norway in October and had haunted the coast since then. Because he frequently hunted by day, and his wings were long, some mistook him for a hawk, but his short tail and big head gave him away.

He beat up to the end of the field without success, then angled back with the wind to hunt a fresh quarter. Rolling, pitching and yawing, he came up to the field like a drunken sailor, this time to lift over the fence to continue over the stubble beyond.

Suddenly he pounced, and rose almost immediately with a meadow pipit which had covered on his approach, hoping that he would pass.

He flew on with his prey to the sheltered side of a rough bank and flopped there. Unlike Kek, he would make no attempt to pluck his victim, but would swallow it whole, for he had a prodigious gape, and would later eject its remains as a rounded pellet of feathers and bones.

Meanwhile, Kek had taken half a dozen pitches without success. Not that he had missed anything. Unlike human sight, which could only focus sharply on one small object at a time, the kestrel's eyes were so designed that almost the whole of his retinas, the photosensitive 'screens', were in the image plane, and at fifty feet the ground below, within a wide angle, was in needle sharp focus. His retinas had three times the density of cones – the tiny nerve cells which resolve detail – that humans have, so that even a small beetle crawling on a blade of grass fifty feet below could be detected.

But no beetle crawled, nor mouse stirred. He was keenly aware of other creatures, but also knew that they were aware of him; that it would be futile to drop. The little Lapland buntings, for instance, which ran and sometimes hopped over the snow by the fence, leaving a trail of prints characterized by the mark of the long hind claw. They rose with a protesting 'ticky-tick-tu' when he pitched above them, and flew over to the seaweed covered rocks to join a band of snow bunting that drifted, almost aimlessly, like blown spume.

He continued to work patiently and methodically into the wind. Two fields away a great flock of larks and meadow pipits foraged downwind. The hard weather had banded them together hundreds strong, and now they gleaned their way greedily across the snow covered stubble, the sea birds rising to fly low over the heads of the birds in front so that they became leaders. In this way, like an ever rolling carpet, they came nearer to the wary kestrel, who had risen to a hundred feet above the dyke between stubble and rough field.

When the first birds reached the dyke he dropped like a plummet, flattening out on protesting wings just before he hit the ground, and struck with full fury among them. As they rose with alarmed cries it seemed that he had collided with a lark and missed; but he continued his fast flight across wind with the bird hanging limply from a drooped talon.

The lark was fairly plump and made a satisfying meal, so he sat quietly for a while on the earthen dyke top where he had plucked and eaten it.

An hour later he had worked his way half a mile up the coast, and now sat on a coast guard lookout tower. The wind had changed to the south east and it was definitely warmer.

Already the snow
on the steep
banks below the
tower had almost
melted away, and
a heavy mist
rolled in from the
sea.

The tower
overlooked a fine
mussel bed which
was haunted by
many shore birds when it was uncovered, and by mollusc
eating diving ducks at high tide. Now, huge breakers
thundered across it, and the waders had retired to rocky islets
to wait the turn of the tide. Fifty yards out, a raft of common
scoters displayed their exquisite seamanship as they buoyantly
rode the waves. From out of the grey mist, the long swell
would build up into a great green eight foot wall of water
which would roll down upon the little black ducks, who had
its nature judged to perfection. Sometimes they would
nonchalantly allow themselves to be lifted up and over, to
disappear in the deep trough behind the wave; then to
reappear in calm water as it toppled and thundered away
from them.

At other times the roller was glassy walled and white
crested: then, as it reared above them ready to smash down
upon them, they would flick out of sight through it, a split
second before the crest curved over and the wall disintegrated
with a roar and a hiss of boiling surf.

Further out, where the swell first became visible, a lone bird fished. It was just a grey silhouette, in outline, not unlike a cormorant, but more streamlined, with a slight up tilted effect to the long dagger-like beak, produced by an upward slope of the lower mandible. It was a red throated diver, not aptly named at this time of year, for in winter it was white throated. The diver disappeared smoothly beneath the swell and his long underwater hunt took him fifty yards out to sea so that when he surfaced the mist now hid him from view.

The mist closed in further, and the scoter became vague shapes, then vanished. Kek shivered his wings to shake off the tiny droplets of moisture that condensed on his feathers, excreted, then launched off the tower and winnowed down the coast, back to the fields behind the mist shrouded lighthouse.

He had the area mapped and memorized: the urge to explore had left him and, instinctively, he knew that this was the place for his winter quarters.

8

The birds around me hopped and played,
Their thoughts I cannot measure:–
But the least motion which they made
It seemed a thrill of pleasure.

Lines Written in Early Spring, William Wordsworth

One morning early in March, the kestrel saw the partridge covey break up. They had been restless for days and the kestrel felt it too. This morning had more than a hint of spring. Heavy dew on the hawthorn bushes shimmered in the sun's horizontal rays and from far across the field came the throb of the peewit wings as they tumbled in gleeful display. Somewhere a tractor started up.

The partridges had formed a wide, loose circle where the males ran at astonishing speeds in their courtship display. It would not be many days before only pairs of the birds whirred up from the stubble into the sky.

Kek caught a vole which he took to the top of a telegraph pole to eat: afterwards he sat there for a few minutes, head withdrawn to his shoulders, soft flank feathers fluffed about his tarsus, leaving only the strong yellow toes showing.

Then, as if he had made a sudden decision, he dropped into a long, stiff winged glide and swung down the coast in a southerly direction. A few minutes of alternate gliding and easy winnowing of his wing tips brought him over the north pier, and he slid into the harbour.

A line of black cormorants drying their wings in the breeze

stood on the Black
Midden rocks, which
in days gone by had
claimed many a
good ship. Black-
headed gulls wheeled
about. They actually
had chocolate brown
heads and it was
only at a distance
they looked black.
Among them,
however, was one

whose head was truly black, with wing tips as white as snow.
This was a Mediterranean gull, a great rarity.

The kestrel flew over the hailing station and past the old
lighthouses and fishing fleet where a herring gull made a
spiteful pass at him. Although it would be another year before
he became fully adult, he was easily mistaken for one now.

He was certainly treated as one as he passed the first
shipyard on the north bank. An angry chattering blue-tailed
male shot from below a jib and chivied him, until he flung
himself low to swing up-river by the south bank. When he
came to an elbow in the river and flew over a mud bank, a
noisy skirmish was taking place above him – harsh and
raucous cawing, shrill kekking and shrill kee-kee-keeing
mingled with the clamour of the shipyard on the opposite
bank. He didn't recognise his parents, but only knew
instinctively that he was unwanted here.

Kek flew on, urged by feelings he had never experienced
before, between the sprawling, grimy towns on each side of

the river, past Newcastle with its busy quay and under the tall bridges that spanned it. He flew on to the end of the tidal reaches where the river banks were less steep and bright coltsfoot grew among the cinders by the riverside railway lines. On he flew until the river bed broke the surface and the sparkling water began to sing on the stones. Beyond the rapids lay the deep pools where the brown trout lurked.

He flew above these and seared a kingfisher who flew like a shaft of living light from his catkin hung perch.

Relieved of the lovely bird's weight, the hazel rod sprung up and tossed its heavy yellow catkins in the breeze. The dusty pollen scattered: most of it was wasted and drifted to the river, but it needed only one tiny grain to settle on the inconspicuous female flowers that studded the upper sides of the shoots. Kek glided down to a post on the low river bank and pitched there. The river had recently been flooded and the adjoining meadow was wet and rushy. In the sheltered corner a tall, grey backed bird with an S-curved neck stalked without splash or ripple in the pools. Kek had never seen a heron before and he nodded curiously as he watched it.

The long, curved neck suddenly straightened and the dagger beak shot out to impale a frog, newly out of hibernation. It was swallowed with a toss of the head. The heron's yellow rimmed eye was expressionless; there was something quite impartial about the incident.

It continued its graceful, silent stalk by a muddy ditch. Again the beak shot out like a crossbow bolt, and was withdrawn quickly with a writhing eel about it. The eel was dumped on a dry bank and stabbed and thumped into submission; then was swallowed.

To Kek's right a water vole splashed in a flood filled ditch. The sights and sounds of food pushed aside his urge to fly on, and he launched himself and took a low pitch above a patch of rushes.

Ten miles away, a hen kestrel sat on the dead branch of a pine above a sixty foot shale cliff. Below was a peat-brown burn which had its source in a flat, green moss bog, a mile away on the high moor. The hen kestrel had lived in this valley with her mate for four seasons, and now, at the end of winter, she had watched her mate die.

He had eaten a rat, caught behind the cowsheds at a farm on the hillside. Shortly after she had screamed at him as he writhed on a ledge on the cliff face. He had made as if to fly down to the water, had toppled in mid air, fallen to the sloping shale, and he lay there now, one wing in the burn. How could he have known that the rat had eaten a poisoned meal: that when he caught it, it was running in agony to the ditch to try to wash away the fire inside it?

The hen flew down to the limp body, curious yet fearful of it. This was not part of the idle display that he had lately indulged in. She kek-kek-kekked, as she glided, stiff winged, down to him and landed among panicles of butterbur. A breeze blew his other wing which rested on rushes. She panicked and kekked and leapt into flight to climb the cliff.

Kee-kee-kee, the shrill voice of a cock kestrel rang in the valley, and joyously she answered and hurled herself into a tremendous whirlpool of flight around and over the cliff.

But suddenly she realized that this was not her mate. This was some bar tailed usurper. He voice changed to brittle anger as she hurled herself down upon Kek who slid easily away, towered on rapidly winnowing wings then dived for a dark fir

wood a quarter of a mile up-stream. She gave
up the chase and circled to land on the
rotten pine limb. Her mate lay still
with the murmuring burn.

That night it rained heavily on
the moors. The moss swelled
quickly, like a giant sponge as
it tried to absorb the rain.
But, within minutes, the
gentle burn became a
raging brown torrent
that thundered over
the ten foot fall
below the fir wood.

Behind the
cascade, a
dipper slept in a
huge, domed,
mossy nest.
Next
morning,
the dipper
plunged
through the

watery curtain to feed, returning with a beak full of beech
leaves to line the nest. The breeze from the fell brought with it
the liquid call of the curlew, and the river tinkled in tune with
the dipper's song.

Kek was up and about early, circling high over the cliff. He
could see the female perched morosely on the pine branch. He
had never attempted something like this before, but something

prompted him. Stoop, stoop, stoop, it urged; but not to kill.

He slid down smoothly in a long dive, pulling out twenty feet above the pine, and climbed rapidly. He wheeled and dived again, this time to fling himself sideways and lopped away when only ten feet in front of the female. His third stoop had the recklessness of youth – he almost knocked her from her perch and she chattered in anger. Or was it anger? Together they rose and swirled, and again he sought refuge in the fir wood, frightening from it a flock of grey-rumped fieldfares. Bird song was everywhere. Strangely, all the songs stimulated every species and the kestrel too felt the urge to court the female more intensely. He followed her when she climbed out of the valley and began to hunt over the fields, keeping a respectful distance. When they had gorged themselves he circled above her as she returned to the valley, to pitch on her favourite perch. All day he paid court to her, and after their evening meal, when she had landed on her roosting ledge on the cliff, he settled on a ledge not many feet away. To this she did not object.

Dusk enveloped the valley and a brown owl hooted. A full moon threw the cliff face into a deep shadow. From a black hole in the sandy bank, a boar badger tested the air and finding all well he drew himself fully out of the sett entrance followed by his family. A hedgehog snuffled over the badger tracks and retreated hurriedly as his wet nose detected the badger spoor.

The moon drifted across the sky and softly illuminated the shale cliff. The two kestrels sat huddled on their ledges next to each other, fast asleep with their heads tucked under their mantle feathers. An exciting new dawn was awaiting them, and the river Tyne.

An oil sketch of the artist and naturalist James Alder by his friend John Gilroy, painted shortly before Gilroy's death in 1985.

James was modelling Kek for Royal Worcester.

James Alder's passion for nature

My father, James Alder (1920-2007), was born in Newcastle where he attended the Royal Jubilee School near the banks of the Tyne. His artistic talents were recognised early, and he was given a one man exhibition at just thirteen years of age.

After winning a scholarship to King's College, Newcastle, he joined the art department at *Newcastle Evening Chronicle*. and for twenty years he wrote and illustrated a very popular nature column for the newspaper.

In addition to his bird, animal and flower painting, James illustrated many books and was a creative advertising designer and sculptor, working with Royal Worcester in porcelain and bronze. He was awarded an honorary Masters Degree and a Doctorate from the University of Newcastle and, as his final accolade, he was appointed President of The Northumberland and Durham Natural History Society.

Some of his finest works are to be seen in his two books, *The Birds of Balmoral* which he wrote for HM Queen Elizabeth II, and *The Birds and Flowers of the Castle of Mey* which he wrote for HM The Queen Mother. His final work was a large watercolour painting of the Wild Cattle of Chillingham.

My father wrote this story, with a working title of *Kek*, in the 1950s, but it was only after his death that I discovered the loose and incomplete type-written pages. Many pages were missing altogether. I do clearly remember the young kestrel that came to stay with us when I was a little boy, and especially its reaction to our hamster!

Over several weeks, in the Spring of 1953, James recorded and photographed the activities of a kestrel family that had nested in tower No. 8 at Walker Naval Yard on the Tyne. The resulting story was published in two features in the *Evening Chronicle* and written up for the Swan Hunter Year Book. James also cared at his home for one of the chicks, which had unfortunately fallen into a bucket of machine oil, until the young bird was ready to return to the wild.

Having some skill as an artist, I decided to complete and illustrate the original text which so vividly describes the natural history of the Tyne and the North Sea shore, incorporating some of my father's original drawings and photographs. I am sure he would have approved.

Rod Alder, 2014

The Wild Cattle of Chillingham by James Alder.

James Alder's beautiful painting of a kestrel (falco tinnunculus) from the artwork (reduced) for his book Birds and Flowers of the Castle of Mey, 1993.

Newcastle Libraries

A bird's eye view of the Naval Yard at Walker, 1962.

Spring 1953, the City of Durban, above, nears completion.

The hide

From eggs to fledglings, Spring 1953.

James Alder

James Alder